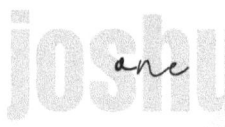

What a promise! What a word! Can you imagine how Joshua must have felt as he stepped into the monumental role of leading the Israelites into the Promised Land, knowing he had God's unwavering support? This divine assurance must have filled his heart with confidence and courage, but he also probably felt a tinge of fear, a little uncertainty.

> "No one will be able to stand against you as long as you live. I will be with you, just as I was with Moses. I will not leave you or abandon you."
> Joshua 1:5 CSB

We can all relate to that mixture of emotions. Whether you're stepping into leadership for the first time, trying something new, or even simply adjusting to new roles in life, it's natural to feel both excitement and concern. The questions arise: *Do I have what it takes? Will I succeed? How will I handle it?* But God, like He did with Joshua, promises to walk with us. The same God who carried Moses was the One who would carry Joshua, and He carries us in the same way today.

"Above all, be strong and very courageous to observe carefully the whole instruction my servant Moses commanded you. Do not turn from it to the right or the left, so that you will have success wherever you go" (Joshua 1:7 CSB). No matter the task, no matter the new season, God gives us the same instruction: *Keep My Word at the center.* When we stay grounded in His Word, meditate on it day and night, and let it guide our decisions, He will be with us.

The Word of God is our foundation. Let's stay focused on it, stay strong, and stay courageous.

As we step into new roles in our lives—leading, growing, and facing new challenges—let's remember that the same God who was with Moses and Joshua is with us too. And with Him, we can do all things.

Prayer:

Lord, thank You for the promise that You are always with me, just as You were with Joshua. Help me prioritize time in Your Word, meditate on it day and night, and trust in Your guidance wherever I go. I'm grateful that You go before me, that You never leave me, and that I can lean on You in every season of life. Lead me, Lord, in the way I should go. In Jesus' name. Amen.

WHAT IS MANNA IN THE MORNING?

In the Old Testament, manna was the food provided to the Israelites as they journeyed through the wilderness to the promised land. It was provided each morning specifically for that day, and if the Israelites tried to store it up, the manna would rot and fill with maggots. It truly was a daily provision from God, just like we believe reading a chapter of the Bible a day is our daily provision from God no matter what we are walking through. No matter how we are feeling, what we are doing, or how we are doing it, God will provide. He will speak to our personal circumstances. One of the things I have found to be true time and time again as I get in God's Word is that no matter how He chooses to speak to me, He never fails to show up.

There is no right or wrong way to use this devotional, but we hope it inspires you to read and study the Word for yourself—to lean in and receive your own revelations from God. We suggest you read the chapter for the day prior to reading the devotional assigned to that chapter. As you begin your time each day, we encourage you to ask the Holy Spirit to speak to you through the Word. We want you to get your own manna in the morning and return daily to get exactly what you need. As you read and sometimes wrestle with the Word each day, we want to encourage you to use the daily companion journal to pray, document, and converse with God about whatever you are reading and thinking.

We can't tell you what will happen as you get in the Word each day, but we can guarantee you that the Lord will show up and blow your socks off. Now grow in grace and the knowledge of our Lord as He reveals His character and develops yours.

welcome

Congratulations and thank you to those of you who have been reading with us daily. We are in books of the Bible that can be difficult and intimidating to read. There is a lot of talk about the Tabernacle and all the rituals required to enter the Lord's presence. It may seem unimportant now, but there are present-day applications in these books of the Bible.

There is so much symbolism for us to unpack. It is very deep and also very exciting. Keep that in mind as we dive in.

joshua

The story of Rahab and how she hid the Israelite spies is absolutely beautiful, but today, let's focus on an aspect of the story we don't usually give much thought to: God's reputation. Rahab's words reveal something profound. When she talks about the Israelites' victory over Sihon, Og, and the Red Sea, it's clear that the entire region had already heard of what God had done. They didn't need to witness the miracles firsthand—they had heard the stories, and God's power was so well-known that it left their enemies trembling.

> "For we have heard how the LORD dried up the water of the Red Sea before you when you came out of Egypt, and what you did to Sihon and Og, the two Amorite kings you completely destroyed across the Jordan. When we heard this, we lost heart, and everyone's courage failed because of you, for the LORD your God is God in heaven above and on earth below."
>
> Joshua 2:10–11 CSB

Sometimes we feel the pressure to speak eloquently or have perfect actions to lead others toward a deeper relationship with the Lord. But let today's reading be a reminder that God's reputation precedes us. We don't have to be perfect or have all the answers. God's goodness, faithfulness, and power are evident in the world around us. He's been at work in ways big and small in our lives. Our job isn't to manufacture that power—it's to share what He's already done.

Just like Rahab, who recognized God's power from the stories she'd heard, people around us can recognize God's power when we share what He has done in our lives. Let's share the challenges we've faced and how God's hand has been at work in the midst of those challenges.

Let's point to His faithfulness even when we don't have all the answers or solutions.

Prayer:

Lord, thank You for the reminder that Your reputation goes before me. Help me share Your goodness in my life and be a living testimony of Your faithfulness. Forgive me for the times I've focused on trying to be perfect or eloquent instead of just sharing what You've done in my life. Help me point others to You in every season of my life and trust that You are at work even when I can't see it. In Jesus' name. Amen.

joshua three

Joshua was a different kind of leader than Moses was. Moses, the diplomat, was known for his patience, humility, and ability to bring peace during times of turmoil. Joshua, however, was more of a military leader—a man of action and decisiveness. Because God's timing and choice were perfect, Joshua was the exact leader the Israelites needed to take them into the Promised Land.

> "The LORD spoke to Joshua: 'Today I will begin to exalt you in the sight of all Israel, so they will know that I will be with you just as I was with Moses.'"
>
> Joshua 3:7 CSB

There are times in life that require patience, diplomacy, and gentleness, like Moses exhibited. And there are times when things need to be shaken up, when action and decisiveness are necessary, like in Joshua's time. The Israelites needed a strong leader who would take charge and lead them into the Promised Land.

Let's be encouraged that God knows exactly what His people need at every stage. He doesn't make mistakes in His appointments or timing. When the challenge calls for a different style of leadership, He provides the right leader for the job.

God promised to be with Joshua, just as He was with Moses. Let this be a reminder that God doesn't leave us to lead or live in our own strength. He goes with us.

Prayer:

Lord, thank You for Your faithfulness in providing exactly what I need in every season of life. Thank You for showing me that You equip me to lead, not in my own strength, but with Yours. Help me embrace the leadership style You've given me and use it for Your glory, whether it's in a moment of patience and diplomacy or in a time of action and decisiveness. May I always trust that You will be with me, just as You were with Moses and Joshua. In Jesus' name. Amen.

joshua four

The memorials built by the tribes of Israel can teach us a few powerful lessons. These stones, placed in the middle of the Jordan River, would forever stand as a testament to God's miraculous intervention. But more than that, they were meant to serve as a reminder to future generations of God's faithfulness.

> "Tell them, 'Take twelve stones from the very place where the priests are standing in the middle of the Jordan. Carry them out and pile them up at the place where you will camp tonight.'"
>
> "We will use these stones to build a memorial. In the future your children will ask you, 'What do these stones mean?'"
>
> Joshua 4:3, 6 NLT

Let today's reading be an encouragement: If God did it for them, He'll do it for us. These stories of God's faithfulness, His miraculous provision, and His mighty hand in the lives of His people should give us hope. We, too, can look back on our own "stones"—times when God moved in powerful ways in our lives—and say, If He did it then, He can do it now.

We can share our stories and build one another's faith. We can remind each other of God's goodness, power, and provision. Whether it's a small victory or a huge miracle, our stories carry the potential to inspire someone else to trust God more deeply. When we share our testimonies, we remind others that they, too, can know that God is working in their lives.

Prayer:

Lord, thank You for Your faithfulness in every season of my life. Thank You for Your miracles and provision, both big and small. Help me be faithful in sharing the stories of Your goodness with others, especially with the next generation. May I be a walking testimony of Your faithfulness, and may I never forget to tell of the great things You've done. May the stories I share build others' faith and inspire them to continue trusting in You. In Jesus' name. Amen.

joshua *five*

So often, when we face challenges, we see them through a human lens: us vs. them, right vs. wrong, win vs. lose. But Joshua's encounter with the commander of the Lord's army reminds us that our battles are not just physical; they are spiritual.

> "When Joshua was near Jericho, he looked up and saw a man standing in front of him with a drawn sword in his hand. Joshua approached him and asked, 'Are you for us or for our enemies?'
>
> "'Neither,' he replied. 'I have now come as commander of the LORD's army.'
>
> "Then Joshua bowed with his face to the ground in homage and asked him, 'What does my lord want to say to his servant?'
>
> "The commander of the LORD's army said to Joshua, 'Remove the sandals from your feet, for the place where you are standing is holy.' And Joshua did that."
>
> Joshua 5:13–15 CSB

"For our struggle is not against flesh and blood, but against the rulers, against the authorities, against the powers of this dark world and against the spiritual forces of evil in the heavenly realms" (Ephesians 6:12 NIV).

Joshua was preparing for war, but God was calling him to surrender. The first command wasn't about battle tactics but about recognizing God's presence: "Remove the sandals from your feet, for the place where you are standing is holy."

When we face battles, we must remember that the Lord fights for us. He does the heavy lifting. We are not to strive in our own strength but to trust in His power.

Victory isn't found in our strategy but in our surrender to Him.

Prayer:

Father, help me see my battles through Your eyes. Remind me that I am not fighting against flesh and blood but that my real battles are spiritual. Teach me to surrender, to trust, and to stand firm in faith, knowing that You fight for me. Thank You for carrying the weight that I cannot. In Jesus' name. Amen.

joshua six

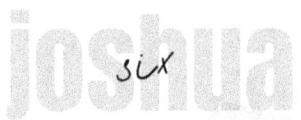

Sometimes the Lord will place something on our hearts—an instruction, a calling, or even a simple prompting—and it will feel completely foolish. Sharing what God has told us to do with others, or even just stepping out in obedience, can feel intimidating at times. God's ways are not our ways. His plans often look nothing like what we expect, and they rarely make sense to the world.

> "The seventh time around, as the priests sounded the long blast on their horns, Joshua commanded the people, 'Shout! For the LORD has given you the town! Jericho and everything in it must be completely destroyed as an offering to the LORD. Only Rahab the prostitute and the others in her house will be spared, for she protected our spies.'
>
> "So the LORD was with Joshua, and his reputation spread throughout the land."
>
> Joshua 6:16–17, 27 NLT

Can you imagine how Joshua felt as he led the Israelites in marching around the town of Jericho? Do you think he wrestled with doubt—questioned how walking in silence for six days and then shouting on the seventh could possibly bring down fortified walls? Regardless of how he felt, he obeyed. And because he did, God moved, and miracles took place.

Then, there's Rahab—a woman whose past as a prostitute should have disqualified her by human standards, yet she is remembered for whom she trusted. Her faith led to her redemption, and she became part of the lineage of Christ.

God is not limited by our past, nor is He constrained by human logic.

When we follow Him, even when it feels foolish, He is glorified.

Prayer:

Father, thank You for reminding me that Your ways are higher than mine. Help me to trust You even when obedience feels foolish. Give me the courage to follow where You lead, knowing that You are faithful. Thank You for redeeming my past and using me for Your glory. Let my life be a testimony of what You can do through those who trust and obey You. In Jesus' name. Amen.

joshua *seven*

This passage seems so intense—almost barbaric. Can you imagine the weight of that moment, the fear that must have swept over the camp? Achan's punishment was severe, but it wasn't without purpose. It was a clear message about the seriousness of sin and the importance of obedience to God.

> "Joshua said, 'Why have you brought us trouble? Today the LORD will bring you trouble!' So all Israel stoned them to death. They burned their bodies, threw stones on them..."
>
> Joshua 7:25 CSB

Let today's reading stir in our hearts gratitude for the grace we now have through Christ. Under the Old Covenant, sin required swift and severe judgment. Under the New Covenant, Jesus took that judgment upon Himself. The punishment we deserve, He bore. The stones that should have been for us fell on Him instead.

Oh, the gravity of sin—it separates us from God and carries real consequences. But it also magnifies the beauty of grace. Because of Jesus, we are not condemned; we are forgiven. The call to obedience is just as important today as it was in Joshua's time, but instead of being driven by fear, we are compelled by love—love for the One who gave everything to redeem us.

Prayer:

Father, thank You for the grace that covers me. I don't take lightly the weight of sin or the cost of disobedience, but I stand in awe of the mercy You have shown through Christ. Help me to walk in obedience, not out of fear but out of love and gratitude for what Jesus has done. Thank You for the New Covenant, for redemption, and for the freedom found in You. In Jesus' name. Amen.

joshua *eight*

Joshua didn't read "some" of what Moses commanded; he read it all.

> "There was not a word of all that Moses had commanded that Joshua did not read before the entire assembly of Israel, including the women, the dependents, and the resident aliens who lived among them."
>
> Joshua 8:35 CSB

Partial obedience is disobedience. Joshua's faithfulness in doing everything the Lord commanded is a challenge to us. How often do we obey only the parts of God's instructions that are comfortable or convenient? Joshua's thoroughness shows us what it means to be fully surrendered and operate in full obedience.

While reading this chapter, you may have found yourself wondering why God allowed Israel to take plunder from Ai when He prohibited it in Jericho. Let this be a reminder that God's instructions are His to give. What He forbids in one season, He may allow in another. The key is trusting that His ways are higher, even when we don't fully understand.

Prayer:

Father, thank You for being the God of second chances. When I fail, help me listen to Your voice and walk in obedience, confident that You've gone before me. Give me the courage to try again when You call me to, and help me be faithful in following every detail of Your Word. I surrender to Your ways, even when they don't make sense to me. In Jesus' name. Amen.

joshua *nine*

The Gibeonites had heard of the Lord's mighty works, and it moved them to action. Their fear wasn't just about survival—it was recognition of God's unmatched power. They knew He was sovereign, and that realization led them to surrender.

> "They answered Joshua, 'Your servants were clearly told how the LORD your God had commanded his servant Moses to give you the whole land and to wipe out all its inhabitants from before you. So we feared for our lives because of you, and that is why we did this. We are now in your hands. Do to us whatever seems good and right to you.'"
>
> Joshua 9:24–25 NIV

This kind of reverence is not about being afraid of God but about truly seeing Him for who He is: holy, powerful, and worthy of all honor. When we grasp the greatness of God, it should stir something in us—a desire to obey, to trust, and to follow wherever He leads. True reverence leads to worship, not just with our words, but with our lives.

Reverence isn't about fear that pushes us away. It's about awe. It's about wonder. And that draws us closer.

Prayer:

Father, help me to see You rightly. Give me a heart that reveres You, not with fear that keeps me at a distance but with a deep awe that stirs my obedience and trust. May my life be a reflection of the worship You are worthy of. In Jesus' name. Amen.

joshua ten

Integrity is a rare quality, especially when the stakes are high. The Gibeonites had deceived Joshua and the Israelites, yet when they were in need, Joshua chose to honor his word. Even though the Gibeonites had tricked him, humiliating him by turning back on their word, Joshua understood that his commitment to them was a reflection of him, not them.

> "The Gibeonites then sent word to Joshua in the camp at Gilgal: 'Do not abandon your servants. Come up to us quickly and save us! Help us, because all the Amorite kings from the hill country have joined forces against us.'
> "So Joshua marched up from Gilgal with his entire army, including all the best fighting men."
>
> Joshua 10:6–8 NIV

When we are people of integrity, we honor our commitments no matter how difficult or inconvenient they may be. It's easy to break promises when circumstances change, but true integrity means standing firm and doing what we've said we'll do, even when it's challenging. Joshua's decision to keep his word wasn't just about following through—it was about showing God's character to the world.

Integrity leads us to act with honor, even when others might not. And when we stand firm in our commitments, God stands with us, guiding and strengthening us through the challenges.

Prayer:

Father, help me be a person of integrity, honoring my word even when it's hard. Give me the strength to follow through on every promise I make, knowing that my commitments reflect You. Teach me to trust that when I choose integrity, You fight alongside me. In Jesus' name. Amen.

joshua eleven

Today, we see that God's promises are not dependent on our perfection or our faithfulness but on His. The Israelites had their failures. Moses, though a servant of God, was not without flaw. Even Joshua, who served so well, had his moments of weakness. Yet, despite all of this, God's promise to His people was fulfilled.

> "Joshua took control of the whole land of Israel as the LORD had told Moses long ago. The Lord gave that land to Israel as he promised. And Joshua divided the land among the tribes of Israel. Finally, the fighting ended and there was peace in the land."
>
> Joshua 11:23 ERV

The fulfillment of this promise was not because of the Israelites' perfect obedience but because of God's unwavering faithfulness to do what He said He would do. God is who He says He is. He is faithful, and His character is unchanging. Even when we fall short, He remains true to His Word.

Prayer:

Lord, thank You for Your unfailing faithfulness. I am grateful that Your promises are not dependent on my perfection but on Your character. Help me to trust in who You are, not in my own ability. Thank You for fulfilling Your promises, for fighting on my behalf, and for showing Your faithfulness in every season. May I rest in the assurance that You are always true to Your Word. In Jesus' name. Amen.

Today, we see an incredible record of victory: The Israelites defeated thirty-one kings. That number isn't just a statistic; it's a testament to the power of God working through Joshua and the Israelites. This is not just about military victories or conquests—it's about God's mighty hand moving through Joshua and the Israelites.

> "In all, thirty-one kings were defeated."
>
> Joshua 12:24 NLT

Joshua's leadership was not about his own strength or wisdom. The victories came because of God's faithfulness and power, and Joshua understood that. Every victory was a reflection of the Lord's greatness, not his own. With every battle they fought, God's reputation grew, and the nations surrounding Israel began to hear of His mighty works.

What a powerful reminder that our lives should be a reflection of God's power and faithfulness. As Jesus' followers, our lives should be a reflection to our communities and beyond of the God we serve.

We may not be leading armies or defeating kings, but God's power and glory should be seen in how we live, how we trust, and how we follow Him. Our faithfulness and obedience give God the opportunity to work through us.

Prayer:

Lord, help me live in a way that reflects Your greatness and builds Your reputation. May my life be a testament to Your faithfulness and power. Thank You for the opportunities You give me to bring glory to Your name. In Jesus' name. Amen.

twelve

Prayer:

Lord, help me live in a way that reflects Your greatness and builds Your reputation. May my life be a testament to Your faithfulness and power. Thank You for the opportunities You give me to bring glory to Your name. In Jesus' name. Amen.

 Listen to "Famous For (I Believe)" by Christine D'Clario and Tauren Wells

thirteen

Joshua, though old in years, is reminded by God that there is still much to be done. His role in God's plan was not yet finished—the land was not fully possessed.

> "Joshua was now old, advanced in age, and the LORD said to him, 'You have become old, advanced in age, but a great deal of the land remains to be possessed.'"
>
> Joshua 13:1 CSB

No matter what stage of life you are in, there is still more for you to do. Whether you've walked closely with the Lord, serving Him for decades, or have been far from Him for years, your story isn't over. The Lord is still working, and He isn't through with you yet.

If you feel like you've wasted time or your best years are behind you, let this be a reminder that God still has plans for you. It's never too late to step into what He has for you. God has work for you, no matter where you are on your journey.

Prayer:

Lord, thank You for Your grace that covers all my years, both the faithful and unfaithful ones. Remind me that You are never finished with me and that You always have more for me to do for Your Kingdom. Help me see that my past does not disqualify me from Your plans. In Jesus' name. Amen.

joshua *fourteen*

Have you ever asked yourself, or even asked the Lord, "How much longer?" Maybe you're waiting for a promise to be fulfilled or hoping for a breakthrough, and the waiting feels endless.

> "Now then, just as the LORD promised, he has kept me alive for forty-five years since the time he said this to Moses, while Israel moved about in the wilderness. So here I am today, eighty-five years old! I am still as strong today as the day Moses sent me out; I'm just as vigorous to go out to battle now as I was then. Now give me this hill country that the LORD promised me that day. You yourself heard then that the Anakites were there and their cities were large and fortified, but, the LORD helping me, I will drive them out just as he said."
>
> Joshua 14:10–12 NIV

What's striking about Caleb's example is not just that he waited but that his faith didn't grow weak in his waiting. He was just as strong in his resolve at eighty-five as he was at forty when the promise was first given. How often do we allow time to shake our confidence and wear down our hope? Caleb's story reminds us that God is faithful even when the wait is long. His promises stand firm no matter the obstacles, no matter the years.

When you're feeling tired of waiting, ask God for the strength to endure, knowing that His timing is perfect and that He will bring to completion what He has promised.

Prayer:

Lord, I feel the weight of waiting, and I often grow weary in the process. Strengthen my faith, and remind me that You are always working, even when I can't see it. In Jesus' name. Amen.

 Listen to "Wait on You" by Maverick City Music and Elevation Worship

The Israelites' partial obedience—not completely driving out the people in the land—may be something we overlook or consider a "small" thing. After all, they were still able to conquer much of the land, and they didn't completely fail, but the truth is, there are consequences to "partial" obedience. The Jebusites remained in Jerusalem, and their presence would later influence the Israelites in ways they could never have anticipated.

> "But the descendants of Judah could not drive out the Jebusites who lived in Jerusalem. So the Jebusites still live in Jerusalem among the descendants of Judah today."
>
> Joshua 15:63 CSB

Partial obedience is disobedience. God's commands aren't about controlling us or taking away our freedom. They are about protecting and guiding us. When He asks us to do something, whether it makes sense to us or not, it's because He sees the bigger picture. He knows that obedience leads to peace, protection, and blessings.

When we don't fully surrender to God's will, we open the door for unnecessary struggles and spiritual compromise, but when we obey completely, we walk in the safety and security of His perfect plan for us.

Prayer:

Lord, thank You for Your guidance and for the protection that comes with obeying Your commands. Help me to trust You completely, even when I don't understand. Teach me to follow You wholeheartedly, knowing that Your ways are always for my good. May I never settle for partial obedience. In Jesus' name. Amen.

When the Israelites settled into the land God had promised them, they were instructed to completely drive out the Canaanites from the territories they were to possess. The tribe of Ephraim did not fully obey. Instead of clearing the land as God had commanded, they allowed the Canaanites to remain, and they became forced laborers.

> "However, they did not drive out the Canaanites who lived in Gezer. So the Canaanites still live in Ephraim today, but they are forced laborers."
> Joshua 16:10 CSB

This decision to coexist with the enemy, even under the guise of forced labor, may have seemed practical to the Israelites, but it was actually a spiritual compromise.

The Israelites had been called to be set apart, and the Canaanites, with their false gods and sinful practices, were a threat to the Israelites' purity.

It's easy to think that coexisting with our "enemies" or allowing certain compromises in our lives won't hurt us. Perhaps we think we can control what influences us or that the occasional small compromise is harmless. But the truth is that small compromises in our lives lead to big consequences down the road.

When we fail to fully follow God's commands—whether it's in our relationships, our choices, or our attitudes—we leave ourselves susceptible to compromise and influence from things that pull us away from God.

Prayer:

Lord, help me to fully follow Your guidance, even when it's difficult. Show me the areas where I have compromised, and give me the strength to stand completely firm on what You've told me. I trust that Your commands are for my protection and my good. May I honor You with my whole heart. In Jesus' name. Amen.

seventeen

The descendants of Joseph were standing on the edge of the land God had promised them, but instead of moving forward in faith, they hesitated. They saw the iron chariots of the Canaanites in the valley and allowed fear to stop them from fully claiming their inheritance. They even expressed their doubt to Joshua, feeling that the land they had was insufficient because of the perceived strength of their enemies.

> "But the descendants of Joseph said, 'The hill country is not enough for us, and all the Canaanites who inhabit the valley area have iron chariots, both at Beth-shean with its surrounding villages and in the Jezreel Valley.'"
>
> Joshua 17:16 CSB

How often do we let fear stop us from stepping into the promises God has given us? The descendants of Joseph had been given a portion of the land, yet they were unwilling to claim it fully because of the obstacles they faced. They allowed their fear of the Canaanites' iron chariots to overshadow their faith in God's ability to give them victory.

It's easy to look at the "iron chariots" in our lives—the challenges that seem so intimidating—and shrink back. But God has promised us victory, and He has already equipped us to face the battles ahead. Fear causes us to look at what's in front of us and focus on our limitations, but faith looks at the same situation and sees God's faithfulness and power at work.

Prayer:

Lord, help me trust You and not be overcome by fear. Show me the areas in my life where I am hesitant, and give me the courage to step forward in faith. I know You have already given me victory, and I want to walk fully in the promises You have prepared for me. In Jesus' name. Amen.

Joshua had led the people faithfully for years, and now, as they stood before the land God had already given them, they hesitated. Were they tired? Did they feel they had all they needed? Was fear keeping them from fully walking into all God had for them?

> "So Joshua asked the Israelites, 'How long will you delay going out to take possession of the land that the LORD, the God of your ancestors, gave you?'"
> Joshua 18:3 CSB

How often do we find ourselves in the same place? God has opened doors, given direction, and even made His promises clear, yet we hesitate. Maybe fear creeps in, maybe complacency sets in, or maybe we just need a reminder. Joshua understood that leadership isn't just about giving orders—it's about continually casting vision, stirring belief, and calling people forward in faith.

Vision leaks. The Israelites had seen God's faithfulness over and over again, yet they still needed a reminder to move forward. We, too, need voices in our lives that remind us to step into what God has already promised. And as leaders—whether in our families, our friendships, or our communities—we must be willing to encourage and call others forward in faith.

Prayer:

Lord, thank You for Your faithfulness and the promises You have given me. If I am delaying in stepping into what You have for me, give me the courage to move forward. Help me to be a person of influence, speaking life, faith, and vision into those around me. May I remind others, as Joshua did, to step fully into Your plans. In Jesus' name. Amen.

nineteen

The Old Testament can feel overwhelming—full of rules, rituals, and long lists that don't always seem relevant. But as we read about the Israelites finally receiving their promised land, let's remember these words: It is finished.

> "So they finished dividing up the land."
>
> Joshua 19:51 CSB

For years, the Israelites wandered, fought, and waited. And now, the promise was fulfilled. Yet, time and time again, they forgot what God had done, complaining and turning away.

Now, let's look at ourselves. We sit here after the greatest promise—Jesus. We didn't have to fight for our salvation. We live in the reality of His finished work. But do we truly treasure it? Or have we, like Israel, taken it for granted?

The entire Old Testament points to Jesus. And here we are, living in the fulfillment of that promise.

Prayer:

Lord, help me always remember the gift of Your Son, Jesus Christ. Help me live in the fullness of what You have finished. In Jesus' name. Amen.

Why on earth did the Israelites need cities of refuge? Well, imagine this: You're chopping wood, and suddenly, the ax head flies off and hits someone. A tragic accident. But in ancient Israel, before you could even explain, the victim's family, assuming you intentionally killed their loved one, could try to seek justice. What do you do? Run!

> "He is to stay in that city until he stands trial before the assembly and until the death of the high priest serving at that time. Then the one who committed manslaughter may return home to his own city from which he fled."
>
> Joshua 20:6 CSB

But not just anywhere. God, in His wisdom, set up six cities of refuge—safe places where people could go until they stood trial. No instant revenge, no mob justice. Instead, a fair hearing. If it was truly an accident, you could stay there, protected, until the high priest passed away.

God wasn't just making laws—He was making a way for justice and mercy to coexist. The human condition is one of irrationality and high emotions that cloud our judgment. Let the cities of refuge be a reminder that:

- God is the God of protection. His laws aren't arbitrary; they are designed to shield His people.
- Jesus is our ultimate refuge. Just as the cities provided safety, Jesus welcomes us in when we need grace, forgiveness, and a fresh start.
- We can extend grace too. Sometimes we need to pause before reacting, giving others the same mercy God gives us.

joshua twenty

Prayer:

Lord, thank You for being my safe place, my refuge in times of trouble. Help me to trust in Your protection and extend grace to others as You do for me. In Jesus' name. Amen.

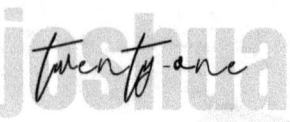

How often do we question God's timing? How often do we wonder if He will come through? Let this be our reminder that God is faithful. He does not forget. He does not change His mind. He does not leave things half-finished.

> "None of the good promises the LORD had made to the house of Israel failed. Everything was fulfilled."
>
> Joshua 21:45 CSB

Wow. Just pause and let that sink in. Every promise God made was fulfilled. Not one failed.

If He said it, He will do it. He can be trusted. Delays are not denials. His timing is perfect. He is the same yesterday, today, and forever. We can trust Him completely. Rest assured, if He said it, He will fulfill it.

Prayer:

Lord, thank You for Your faithfulness. Your promises never fail. Help me to trust in Your timing and rest in the truth that You will do what You have said You will do. In Jesus' name. Amen.

twenty-two

It's easy to see why some of the Israelite tribes were alarmed when they saw an altar being built. They assumed rebellion—turning away from God.

> "What is this treachery you have committed today against the God of Israel...?"
>
> Joshua 22:16 CSB

Isn't it interesting how quickly we assume the worst in others?
Fortunately, instead of acting on assumptions, the Israelites asked questions. They communicated. And because of that, lives were saved.

How often do we jump to conclusions without seeking clarity? How many conflicts could be avoided if we took the time to listen before reacting? What a reminder for us today that communication is vital—not just in leadership but in everyday life.

Prayer:

Lord, help me remember to seek clarification and ask questions before I assume anything. Thank You for Your gentle kindness and for teaching me better ways of communicating. In Jesus' name. Amen.

It's easy to get distracted by fear, by doubt, by the need to know what's coming next. Our minds can wander, questioning what God will do and when. But Joshua's words are a reminder: Stay in the Word. Stay faithful. Stay loyal.

> "Be very strong and continue obeying all that is written in the book of the law of Moses, so that you do not turn from it to the right or left and so that you do not associate with these nations remaining among you. Do not call on the names of their gods or make an oath to them; do not serve them or bow in worship to them. Instead, be loyal to the LORD your God, as you have been to this day."
>
> Joshua 23:6–8 CSB

God never failed the Israelites. Not once. Every single promise He made was fulfilled. And He won't fail us either. Let this resonate in your heart. Let this truth anchor you when your thoughts begin to drift.

Prayer:

Lord, thank You for Your Word. It is a constant reminder of Your faithfulness and character. Keep my heart loyal and my steps steady in You. In Jesus' name. Amen.

twenty-four

You may read verses like this and think, Of course, I wouldn't serve other gods. But we must be careful. Idols can be sneaky. We may not be bowing to statues, but there could be gods we put before the one true God, like the god of self-reliance, for example. It's easy to slip into I-have-to-figure-this-out-myself mode. It's easy to feel alone, like we carry the weight of everything on our shoulders.

> "The people replied, 'We will certainly not abandon the LORD to worship other gods! For the LORD our God brought us and our ancestors out of the land of Egypt, out of the place of slavery, and performed these great signs before our eyes. He also protected us all along the way we went and among all the peoples whose lands we traveled through.'"
> Joshua 24:16–17 CSB

We are never alone, though. The same God who brought the Israelites out of Egypt is the One who leads us, protects us, and provides for us. We don't have to rely on ourselves. He is with us, and we can rely on Him.

Prayer:

Lord, I confess that I often try to do life on my own. Help me trust You more, release control, and lean on You instead of my own strength. Thank You for always being faithful. In Jesus' name. Amen.

judges one

Psalm 46 says that the Lord is an ever-present help, but sometimes we forget to ask. Before stepping into battle, the Israelites didn't assume or strategize on their own. They asked the Lord, and He answered. Not only did the Lord tell them they would get the victory, but He gave them the strategy too.

> "After the death of Joshua, the Israelites asked the LORD, 'Who of us is to go up first to fight against the Canaanites?'
> "The LORD answered, 'Judah shall go up; I have given the land into their hands.'"
>
> Judges 1:1–2 NIV

How often do we try to figure things out ourselves? How many times have we worried, wrestled, or feared the unknown before taking our concerns to the Lord? How many battles have we gone into and through without ever consulting Him?

How silly are we when we don't even consider the Lord, let alone ask Him for the plan and strategy?! God is ready and willing to guide us if we would just ask.

Prayer:

Lord, forgive me for the times I rushed ahead without asking for Your direction. Help me remember to seek Your guidance before taking action. Thank You for Your love and patience. In Jesus' name. Amen.

judges two

It's wild how quickly we move on. God answers a prayer, opens a door, provides a way only He could...and life keeps going without us ever stopping to celebrate. The Israelites had seen God's power, but somehow, the next generation forgot about it. Why? Because no one had talked about it.

> "That whole generation also died, and the next generation forgot the LORD and what he had done for Israel."
>
> Judges 2:10 GNT

Let's not be quiet about what God has done in our lives. Let's not be so focused on what's next that we fail to pass down the stories of His faithfulness. There is so much value in sharing our victories, our struggles, and even the times our stupidity should have taken us out, but God was still faithful. These stories build faith. They remind us of who God is. And they leave a legacy that points back to Him.

Prayer:

Lord, help me be loud about Your goodness. Help me tell the next generation what You've done—not just in the Bible but in my own life. Remind me not to move on too quickly. Give me a heart that remembers and a voice that shares. In Jesus' name. Amen.

judges three

Israel's downfall wasn't some big, catastrophic mistake. It wasn't a huge fallout. It began with a "small" act of disobedience. They didn't fully obey God's command to drive out the other nations as they conquered new land and territory. Instead, they intermarried, and when they intermarried, they were influenced to worship other gods. What started as a "small" compromise led to much bigger consequences.

> "They were to be a test for Israel, to find out whether or not the Israelites would obey the commands that the LORD had given their ancestors through Moses.
>
> "They intermarried with them and worshiped their gods."
>
> Judges 3:4, 6 GNT

God doesn't give us commands to restrict us; He gives us commands to protect us. When we choose partial obedience, it can seem harmless at first, but it often leads to regret and bigger consequences down the road.

Prayer:

Lord, help me trust Your commands and follow them fully. Keep me from compromising and remind me that Your ways are always for my good. In Jesus' name. Amen.

judges four

Don't you love how God's plans rarely (if ever) fit our logic?! The world tells us strength, status, and strategy win battles. But God? He flips that upside down every time.

> "When Barak attacked with his army, the LORD threw Sisera into confusion together with all his chariots and men. Sisera got down from his chariot and fled on foot."
> Judges 4:15 GNT

Sisera rolled in with iron chariots, the ancient-world equivalent of a high-tech military advantage. Israel should have been outmatched, outnumbered, and overpowered. But God didn't need chariots. He didn't need a bigger army. He had already decided the outcome. In a moment, He turned everything around, and the mighty warrior Sisera? He went running for his life. This is just another reminder that God doesn't operate by human logic. He uses foolish things to shame the wise (1 Corinthians 1:27).

God doesn't need what the world considers powerful—He just needs willing hearts. So, if He calls you to something, know that He will bring you through it. It won't always look the way you expect, but it will always be exactly how He intended.

Prayer:

Lord, I don't want to trust in what looks strong—I want to trust in You. Your ways are higher, and You never fail. Help me stop looking at the battle and start looking at the One who's already won. In Jesus' name. Amen.

judges five

What a battle we saw in Judges 4. And not just any battle—an unexpected victory led by an unexpected leader. Even though not everyone showed up, Israel had the upper hand. Some answered the call and fought under Deborah. Others stayed behind. We don't have all the answers as to why, but we do know that God still got the victory.

> "Gilead remained across the Jordan; And why did Dan stay on ships? Asher sat at the seashore, And remained by its landings."
>
> Judges 5:17 NASB

How often do we think, If I don't do this, ____ won't happen? Let today's reading be a reminder that God's plans will always prevail. We just get to decide whether we'll be part of the story or sit on the sidelines.

And then there's Deborah. A woman. A leader. A prophetess. In a time when voices like hers weren't expected—or always welcomed—she stepped up. No hesitation. No excuses. And God used her to bring victory.

Maybe you've felt overlooked, unqualified, or out of place. Maybe you've believed the lie that God only calls certain kinds of people. Let this story remind us that God calls who He calls, and He equips who He calls. He doesn't need us, but He wants us. He chooses us!

The question is—will we say yes? Or will we stay in the harbor, watching from a distance?

judges five

Prayer:

Lord, Your plans never fail, and You don't need me, but You invite me. Thank You for calling the unexpected and using the overlooked. I don't want to miss out. Give me the courage to step into what You're doing, even when it feels uncertain. I say yes to You. In Jesus' name. Amen.

judges six

> "Gideon replied, 'But Lord, how can I rescue Israel? My clan is the weakest in the tribe of Manasseh, and I am the least important member of my family.'
> "The LORD answered, 'You can do it because I will help you. You will crush the Midianites as easily as if they were only one man.'"
>
> Judges 6:15–16 GNT

Does this sound familiar?

I don't have enough time.
I'm too busy.
I don't have the right skills.
It's just me!

Here's the thing: God never asked Gideon to do it alone. And He's not asking you to either. When the Lord calls us, He equips us. When He sends, He goes with us. It's never about our ability—it is always about God's presence.

So, if you're sitting on an assignment God has put on your heart, waiting until you feel "ready," "supported," or "qualified," let this be your reminder: You can do it because He will help you. No more excuses. Let's go.

Prayer:

Lord, I let my excuses hold me back way too often. Help me stop focusing on what I lack and start focusing on You. You are my strength, my help, and my confidence. If You've called me to it, I know You'll bring me through it. In Jesus' name. Amen.

judges five

Prayer:

Lord, Your plans never fail, and You don't need me, but You invite me. Thank You for calling the unexpected and using the overlooked. I don't want to miss out. Give me the courage to step into what You're doing, even when it feels uncertain. I say yes to You. In Jesus' name. Amen.

judges six

Gideon had a whole list of reasons why he wasn't the guy for the job: He was too weak. Too small. Too insignificant.

> "Gideon replied, 'But Lord, how can I rescue Israel? My clan is the weakest in the tribe of Manasseh, and I am the least important member of my family.'
> "The LORD answered, 'You can do it because I will help you. You will crush the Midianites as easily as if they were only one man.'"
>
> Judges 6:15–16 GNT

Does this sound familiar?

I don't have enough time.
I'm too busy.
I don't have the right skills.
It's just me!

Here's the thing: God never asked Gideon to do it alone. And He's not asking you to either. When the Lord calls us, He equips us. When He sends, He goes with us. It's never about our ability—it is always about God's presence.

So, if you're sitting on an assignment God has put on your heart, waiting until you feel "ready," "supported," or "qualified," let this be your reminder: You can do it because He will help you. No more excuses. Let's go.

Prayer:

Lord, I let my excuses hold me back way too often. Help me stop focusing on what I lack and start focusing on You. You are my strength, my help, and my confidence. If You've called me to it, I know You'll bring me through it. In Jesus' name. Amen.

judges seven

This seems to be a recurring theme in Judges: God doesn't need big numbers, just willing hearts.

> "The LORD said to Gideon, 'You have too many troops for me to hand the Midianites over to them, or else Israel might elevate themselves over me and say, "I saved myself."'"
> Judges 7:2 CSB

Imagine standing before a massive army, outnumbered and outmatched, only to hear God say, "You have too many men." Too many? That's the last thing you'd expect to hear before a battle! But God wasn't interested in numbers—He wanted (and still wants) the glory.

God started narrowing down the troops. First, thousands left. Then, even more until, finally, just 300 men remained to face the Midianites. And guess what? God won the battle. God doesn't need a big army. He doesn't need perfect conditions. He looks for willing hearts that trust Him.

Prayer:

Lord, help me trust You when things don't make sense. Remind me that You don't want my strength—just my surrender. Thank You for including me in what You are doing. In Jesus' name. Amen

judges eight

Gideon literally tore down idols and then somehow ended up making one himself. Why?!

> "Gideon made an ephod from all this and put it in Ophrah, his hometown. Then all Israel prostituted themselves by worshiping it there, and it became a snare to Gideon and his household."
> Judges 8:27 CSB

Was it pride? A lapse in judgment? Did he think he was doing something good?

Whatever it was, it backfired—big time. It became a trap for him and his whole family.

We do the same thing. How many times have we seen God come through only to fall right back into old sins? Little compromises don't seem like a big deal...until they are. Gideon's story is a real gut check: Just because God gives the victory doesn't mean we can take our eyes off Him.

Prayer:

Lord, help me not to lose sight of You. Keep my heart from chasing after idols. In Jesus' name. Amen.

judges *nine*

If there's one thing we should never want to forget, it's that God sees it all—every injustice, every hidden motive, every act of faithfulness and unfaithfulness. He doesn't miss a thing. Abimelech thought he could get away with his wickedness, but in the end, God made sure justice was served.

> "And so it was that God paid Abimelech back for the crime that he committed against his father in killing his seventy brothers. God also made the men of Shechem suffer for their wickedness, just as Jotham, Gideon's son, said they would when he cursed them."
>
> Judges 9:56–57 GNT

In today's reading, we see a tragic story unfold. Abimelech, driven by power and selfish ambition, murders his brothers to claim the throne. The people of Shechem, who supported him, later face God's judgment for their wickedness. This chapter is a brutal reminder that sin hurts everyone, not just the person who commits it. It ripples out, affecting everyone in its path and sometimes on to the next generation.

Here's the thing: God's justice is always balanced with His mercy. He sees the heart of every person, and while there are consequences for our choices, there's always the invitation to return to Him. Let the story of Abimelech be a reminder that we reap what we sow and that God sees all, knows all, and offers forgiveness to all who turn to Him.

Prayer:

Lord, thank You for Your justice and mercy. Help me notice when I am tempted to make selfish choices, and remind me of Your desire for me to be righteous.

May I choose Your ways, knowing that You see and know everything. Give me the wisdom to walk in Your truth, and help me extend grace to others just as You've extended it to me. In Jesus' name. Amen.

judges ten

Imagine if God actually left us to the things we put before Him. The people, the status, the comforts—what if they had to be our rescue when we got in trouble? That's a terrifying thought.

> "Go and cry out to the gods you have chosen. Let them rescue you when you get in trouble."
> Judges 10:14 GNT

The Israelites spent years chasing after other gods. And when trouble came? God called them out: Go ask those gods for help. Brutal. But fair.

When they truly repented, God forgave them. That's His heart. When we turn back to Him, His mercy is already waiting.
So why do we fear God? Why do we picture Him as distant or harsh? He's not. Yes, He gets angry. He gets jealous—because He loves us. But no matter how far we go, He's still a loving Father with arms wide open, waiting for us, His children, to come home.

Prayer:

Lord, open my eyes to anything I've put above You and help me remove it. Please also open my eyes to who You truly are. I don't have to be afraid of You—You are love. Thank You for being a good Father, always calling me back with mercy and grace. In Jesus' name. Amen.

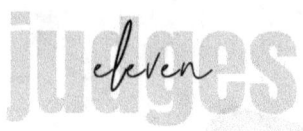

judges eleven

Grief doesn't follow rules. It doesn't fit into a neat little box with a timeline and an expiration date. Just because we don't face it doesn't mean it disappears—it just waits for us down the road.

> "...that the Israelite women would go out for four days every year to grieve for the daughter of Jephthah of Gilead."
> Judges 11:40 GNT

Jephthah's daughter was mourned every year—not just once and forgotten, but remembered. The pain of loss was honored, not ignored. That says something, doesn't it? Grief isn't meant to be rushed past but walked through.

Let's be honest. We don't like sitting in grief. We numb. We avoid. We doom scroll, binge-watch, overeat, overwork, and overspend. We stay busy so we don't have to feel. We reach for temporary fixes instead of the Healer.

Yet Jesus Himself wept. He didn't brush past sorrow or tell people, "Just move on." He felt deeply. And if the Son of God embraced grief, why do we think we should or can skip it?

Maybe today is the day to sit with the Lord and acknowledge what hurts. To stop numbing. To stop pushing it aside. To let Him into that space. Healing doesn't come from avoidance—it comes from facing the pain with the One who heals. When we avoid grief, we're only kicking the can down the road. It will come up, and at some point, it will have to be faced.

Prayer:

Lord, I don't want to keep kicking grief down the road. Show me the things I run to instead of You. Help me sit with You in the hard things—to feel, to process, and to heal. Thank You for being the God who sees, who weeps with me, and who walks me through pain. I trust You with my heart. In Jesus' name. Amen.

judges twelve

Words mattered. A single word—Shibboleth—determined life or death. If they couldn't say it correctly, they didn't belong. Their pronunciation exposed them.

> "The Gileadites captured the fords of the Jordan leading to Ephraim, and whenever a survivor of Ephraim said, 'Let me cross over,' the men of Gilead asked him, 'Are you an Ephraimite?' If he replied, 'No,' they said, 'All right, say 'Shibboleth.' If he said, 'Sibboleth,' because he could not pronounce the word correctly, they seized him and killed him at the fords of the Jordan. Forty-two thousand Ephraimites were killed at that time."
>
> Judges 12:5–6 NIV

How often do we feel like that? Like we have to meet some "standard" to prove we belong? In church, in friendships, in leadership, in the calling God has given us, and even in our own families, we can find ourselves wondering, Do I measure up? Do I fit in?

But here's the truth: God doesn't require perfect pronunciation. He doesn't test us to see if we sound like we belong. He calls us to simply be His, to be faithful, and to follow Him.

Prayer:

Lord, I don't want to live in fear of not measuring up. Thank You that in You, I belong, not because I say the right things or do everything perfectly, but because You call me Yours. Help me to walk in that confidence today. In Jesus' name. Amen.

judges thirteen

Before Samson was even born, he was called. Set apart. Marked for a purpose he didn't choose. His life came with a standard of living he never signed up for.

> "You will become pregnant and give birth to a son, and his hair must never be cut. For he will be dedicated to God as a Nazirite from birth. He will begin to rescue Israel from the Philistines."
> Judges 13:5 NLT

Being called by God sounds exciting, but it can also be uncomfortable. It asks something of us. It costs something.

Samson's calling was clear—dedicated as a Nazirite from birth, separated for God's purpose. His journey wasn't smooth. He didn't always honor the vow meant to empower and protect him, yet God still used him.

What is God asking of you?

Your calling may come with challenges and unanswered questions. It may not look how you expected. But it is an invitation to trust God, to wait on Him, and to follow Him even when you don't see or understand the full picture.

Prayer:

Lord, help me embrace Your calling, even when it stretches me. Forgive me when I try to take control or rush ahead. Help me welcome whatever You have for me, no matter what it looks like. Remind me that it is a privilege to be used by You. May Your Spirit guide me every step of the way. In Jesus' name. Amen.

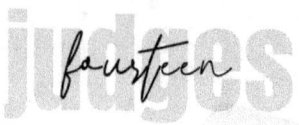

Sometimes, the things we never expect are the ones God uses to fulfill His purpose. Samson's parents couldn't understand why their son wanted to marry a Philistine woman. It made no sense. But what they didn't realize was that God was at work behind the scenes.

> "His father and mother did not know that it was of the LORD, and that He was seeking an occasion [to take action] against the Philistines. Now at that time the Philistines were ruling over Israel."
>
> Judges 14:4 AMP

How often do we assume we know what God would say or do? How many times do we move forward based on our own reasoning, never stopping to ask Him what He actually wants? Proverbs 16:9 reminds us, "A man's heart plans his way, but the Lord directs his steps." Regardless of what we think or want, God's plan always prevails.

This is both humbling and reassuring. Humbling because it reminds us that we should seek His direction, and reassuring because even when we don't seek His direction, He is still in control.

What in your life doesn't make sense right now? Could it be that God is working in ways you don't yet see? Instead of assuming, pause. Ask Him. Trust that His ways are higher than yours.

Prayer:

Lord, forgive me for the times I assume I know Your will without asking. Thank You for directing my steps, even when I don't realize it. Help me trust that You are always working, even when things don't make sense. Give me the wisdom to seek You first. In Jesus' name. Amen.

judges fifteen

Samson was strong, gifted, and chosen by God. But let's be honest—his motives weren't always pure. He wasn't fighting for righteousness here in chapter fifteen; he was fighting for revenge. Yet, God still used him mightily. If God used someone like Samson—flawed, emotional, and often self-focused—then He can use us too. Our past mistakes, our less-than-perfect motives, our weaknesses? They don't disqualify us from God's purpose.

> "Then Samson said to the Philistines, 'You did this bad thing to me, so now I will do bad things to you. Then I will be finished with you!'"
> Judges 15:7 ERV

When we look back at our lives, we may see moments of faithfulness and moments of failure. But here's the good news: God's ability to use us isn't dependent on our perfection. He is bigger than our mistakes. He can take even our messiest moments and turn them into something that points back to Him. He can use our stories for His glory.

Prayer:

Lord, thank You for using imperfect people like me. I know my motives aren't always pure, and I don't always get it right, but I will continue to surrender my life to You. Use me, not because I'm worthy, but because You are. Let my story always point to You. In Jesus' name. Amen.

judges sixteen

Delilah wore Samson down. Day after day, nagging, pleading, pushing until Samson finally caved. He gave up the one thing from God that set him apart, and it cost him everything.

> "Because she nagged him day after day and pleaded with him until she wore him out, he told her the whole truth and said to her, 'My hair has never been cut, because I am a Nazirite to God from birth. If I am shaved, my strength will leave me, and I will become weak and be like any other man.'"
>
> Judges 16:16-17 CSB

But let's be real—Delilah didn't even try to hide her intentions. She straight-up betrayed him multiple times, and he still stayed. Was it pride? Did he think he was too strong to fall? Did he doubt that what God said really mattered? Whatever the reason, he ignored every red flag, and it led to his downfall.

This is a hard truth: What we entertain will either strengthen us or destroy us. If we keep playing with things that God has clearly warned us about, we can't be surprised when they take us out. Samson lost his strength, his calling, and his freedom because he refused to walk away from something toxic.

Prayer:

Lord, help me stop entertaining things that You've already told me to walk away from. Give me wisdom and discernment to see traps and the strength to leave them behind. I don't want to lose what sets me apart. I trust You. In Jesus' name. Amen.

seventeen

Micah wanted to worship, but he knew he needed something or someone to lead him. From what is written, He very much wanted to please the Lord. But without instruction on how to direct his worship, he did whatever made sense to him and placed his hope in idols, a shrine, and a Levite.

> "Then Micah said, 'Now I know that the LORD will be good to me, because a Levite has become my priest.'"
> Judges 17:13 CSB

How can we judge him? Without Jesus as the Leader of our lives and our central focus, we do the same thing. We reach for what makes sense to us—success, relationships, security. Anything to anchor us. But none of it lasts. It can't possibly fill what is missing.

We were made to lean on the Lord, our Shepherd. He is to guide us, lead us, do life with us, and fill the space we try to fill on our own.

Who or what might you be attempting to use to fill the voids in your life that only the Shepherd can fill?

Prayer:

Lord, keep me. Remind me to look to You for safety, rest, peace, hope, courage, and faith. Remind me to forever lean and depend on You. In Jesus' name. Amen.

eighteen

It can be difficult to read how far the Israelites drifted away from God. As a people, they were full of moral corruption, deception, and lawlessness. The Danites had land—God-given land—but they didn't take it. Instead, they went after something easier. Something that required less faith, less fight.

> "The five men left and came to Laish. They saw that the people who were there were living securely, in the same way as the Sidonians, quiet and unsuspecting. There was nothing lacking in the land and no oppressive ruler. They were far from the Sidonians, having no alliance with anyone."
>
> Judges 18:7 CSB

We can be tempted to take the easy way too. It usually seems like a good idea at the moment, but eventually, it catches up with us.

Today's reading is messy, and honestly, so is life sometimes. But even in the mess, God is still there. Even when we take the wrong path or when things feel off, we can be assured He is working behind the scenes. He is for reconciliation and restoration.

Prayer:

Lord, thank You that even in the ugliest, messiest of moments, You are there. You will never leave me, and I will never be alone. Thank You. In Jesus' name. Amen.

nineteen

This chapter is dark—one of the darkest in the Bible. It's easy to wonder, How could God allow something like this?

> "The owner of the house went out and said to them, 'Please don't do this evil, my brothers. After all, this man has come into my house. Don't commit this horrible outrage.'"
> Judges 19:23 CSB

But God gives us free will. He doesn't force us to love Him, follow Him, or choose His ways. And when we serve ourselves instead, this is what happens.

It's disturbing. It's heartbreaking. And it should wake us up.

God's rules aren't about control—they're about protection. He isn't trying to confine us. He wants to keep us safe. When we reject his protection, we don't find freedom. We find destruction.

This is why we need Jesus. When we are left to our own devices, things unravel.

Prayer:

Lord, when I think I know better or could do something better in my own power, please remind me that when I go astray and do things my own way, I make a mess. Help me submit my will to Your will. In Jesus' name. Amen.

judges twenty

The Israelites weren't fighting an enemy nation this time—they were fighting their own people. The thought of facing dear friends and family must have been gut-wrenching, but sin had to be confronted, and boundaries had to be drawn.

> "The Israelites asked, 'Should we again fight against our brothers the Benjaminites or should we stop?'
>
> "The LORD answered, 'Fight, because I will hand them over to you tomorrow.'"
>
> Judges 20:28 CSB

The same is true for us in our lives. Sometimes, the hardest battles we face will be the ones within our own families. Dysfunction, brokenness, and sin don't just go away because we love someone. And while God calls us to be peacemakers, peace doesn't always mean passivity. Sometimes, it means standing firm.

If you're wrestling with setting boundaries, don't do it alone. Seek God's wisdom. He will guide you. Like the Israelites, ask the Lord how to proceed: Should I engage, or should I stop?

Prayer:

Lord, give me discernment to know when to fight and when to step back. Help me set boundaries that honor You and protect my heart. When conflict comes, remind me to seek You first. I trust You to lead me in truth. In Jesus' name. Amen.

twenty-one

After nearly wiping out an entire tribe, you'd think Israel would stop and seek the Lord. But no. Instead, they kept making their own decisions, digging themselves deeper into a mess.

During today's reading, you might have caught yourself wondering, When will they learn?

> "In those days there was no king in Israel; everyone did whatever seemed right to him."
> Judges 21:25 CSB

But a better question is, when will we?

When the Lord is not the center of our lives—when we do not fully surrender to Him—this is where we end up: living life doing whatever seems right at the moment, fixing mistakes with more mistakes, and wondering why things seem so broken.

The truth? We need the King. Not just a ruler, but the Ruler—Jesus. Without Him, we're just as lost as the Israelites were.

Prayer:

Lord Jesus, I need You. There is no doubt about it. On my own and left to my own devices, I know my life would be unmanageable. Lord, help me accept the things I cannot change, change the things I can, and have the wisdom to know the difference. In Jesus' name. Amen.

ruth one

This is covenantal love—the kind of love that stays and commits no matter what. Ruth wasn't just sticking with Naomi out of obligation. She was choosing Naomi—choosing to leave her old life and gods and step into something new for Naomi.

> "But Ruth replied: Don't plead with me to abandon you or to return and not follow you. For wherever you go, I will go, and wherever you live, I will live; your people will be my people, and your God will be my God."
>
> Ruth 1:16 CSB

Covenantal love is:

- **Unbreakable**: A deep commitment, not based on feelings
- **Sacrificial**: Willing to give up everything for another
- **Rooted in faith:** Shows spiritual devotion

Covenantal love isn't about convenience—it's about commitment. It's the same kind of love God has for us. This love says, "I'm not leaving." It adopts, grafts in, and makes outsiders family.
Just like Ruth, we were once outsiders, but through Christ, we've been brought in.

Prayer:

Lord, I have such a hard time truly fathoming covenantal love. I want to understand, and I want to believe in this type of love. Help my unbelief. Thank You for modeling love, Lord. In Jesus' name. Amen.

Boaz doesn't just acknowledge Ruth; he blesses her extravagantly. He sees her, protects her, chooses her, and makes sure she lacks nothing.

> "May the LORD reward you for what you have done, and may you receive a full reward from the LORD God of Israel, under whose wings you have come for refuge."
> Ruth 2:12 CSB

This is a picture of God's love for us. Unearned. Undeserved. Over-the-top extravagant. Fortunately, God doesn't give us what we deserve. Instead, He pours out grace, covering us, protecting us, and calling us His own.

God's love for us goes beyond our expectations and imagination. And when we fully rest in it, we realize that we are seen. We are chosen. We are loved deeply, fully, forever.

Prayer:

Lord, thank You for Your extravagant love. When I don't feel loved, remind me that I am. Help me not just to know Your love but to live in it as well—secure, joyful, and full of grace. In Jesus' name. Amen.

three

Ruth's obedience and trust are mind-blowing. No hesitation. No questioning. Just "I'll do everything you say."

> "So Ruth said to her, 'I will do everything you say.'"
> Ruth 3:5 CSB

You may read this and think, Man, I have so far to go. There might still be some work that needs to be done in our hearts for us to get to this level of trust in and obedience to the Lord, but don't let this be about comparison. Instead, let it be a reminder that we should have a desire for the Lord to shape us, stretch us, and make us more like Ruth in our obedience and trust.

Prayer:

Lord, make me more like Ruth when it comes to obeying and trusting You. Make me willing and loyal. In Jesus' name. Amen.

ruth four

Your experiences may not be the same as Ruth's, but you can probably relate to her longing, her faith, and her hope. Let her story and how God redeemed what she lost encourage you.

> "All the people at the gate and the elders said, 'We are witnesses. May the LORD make the woman who is coming into your house like Rachel and Leah, the two who built the household of Israel. May you achieve wealth and power in Ephrathah and become famous in Bethlehem.'"
> Ruth 4:11 AMP

This is not to say you should expect the same story, but it is to say that you should believe and trust in the same God who authored Ruth's—the God who makes beauty from ashes and takes broken things and restores them in ways you never imagined.

Maybe you're in a season where you don't see a happy ending. Maybe life hasn't turned out the way you thought it would. Let the book of Ruth be a reminder that your story isn't over.

Prayer:

Lord, help me trust You with my story. Remind me that You are writing something beautiful, even while I'm waiting. In Jesus' name. Amen.

1 samuel *one*

Battling infertility can be heartbreaking. The pain of longing for a child and waiting—year after year—without an answer can seem unbearable.

> "'And now I give this child to the LORD. He will serve the LORD all his life.'
>
> "Then Hannah left the boy there and worshiped the LORD."
>
> 1 Samuel 1:28 ERV

When you read about Hannah, you can hear the desperation in her prayers. She begged God for a child, and when He answered, she didn't hold on too tightly—she followed through on her promise and gave Samuel back to Him.

Usually, when we hear about "giving a child to the Lord," we think of dedicating them in prayer and raising them in faith. But Hannah literally left her son at the temple. That level of trust—that kind of faith—should challenge us.

Do you trust God like Hannah, or do you find yourself giving in to the temptation to worry and take control?

Prayer:

Lord, help me be faithful in all things. In the waiting, in the receiving, and in the surrendering. Thank You for always modeling faithfulness. In Jesus' name. Amen.

1 samuel *two*

Hannah's story speaks to a strong faith. After years of waiting and praying for a child, she finally receives the answer to her prayers, only to give her son back to the Lord. Can you imagine the mixed emotions—the joy of receiving God's blessing, followed by the heart-wrenching surrender? In today's reading, we see that she praises God with unshakable joy, declaring that her heart rejoices in Him.

> "Hannah said, 'My heart is happy in the LORD. I feel very strong in my God. I laugh at my enemies. I am very happy in my victory.'"
>
> 1 Samuel 2:1 ERV

What we see in Hannah is that often, the very things we never wanted to go through—the pain, the waiting, the struggle—are the things that shape us the most. Those are the moments that draw us closer to God, helping us understand His heart in ways we never could without walking through the fire.

It's in the hardest moments—when we feel like we can't go any further—that we are forced to lean into God's presence even more. We don't choose the trials we go through, but they can lead to a deeper, more intimate relationship with God.

Prayer:

Lord, help me to trust You in the waiting. Help me see that my suffering is never wasted and always used to bring me closer to You. In Jesus' name. Amen.

1 samuel *three*

You ever hear something and immediately assume you know where it's coming from? That's exactly what happened to Samuel. God was calling him, but he automatically ran to Eli because Eli was the voice of authority in his life.

> "...the LORD called Samuel. He answered, 'Yes, sir!' and ran to Eli and said, 'You called me, and here I am.'
> "But Eli answered, 'I didn't call you; go back to bed.' So Samuel went back to bed."
>
> 1 Samuel 3:4–5 GNT

So much of how we see God is shaped by the people who've led us—parents, pastors, mentors, teachers. And if those people were loving and wise, that's great. But if they were harsh, inconsistent, or absent, it can seriously mess with how we view God.

It can be difficult to separate our experiences with others from who God is. But here's the truth: God is not man. He's not impatient like that one leader who made you feel small. He's not absent like that person who never showed up. He's not unpredictable like the ones who changed the rules on you.

He is steady. He is kind. He is faithful.

And just like Samuel, we have to learn how to recognize His voice for ourselves, not through the filter of people but through who He actually is.

Prayer:

God, I know my view of You has been shaped by people, and honestly, not all of it has been good. Help me unlearn the things that aren't true about You. Teach me to recognize Your voice. Show me who You really are. In Jesus' name. Amen.

1 samuel *four*

The Israelites were so confident when the ark of the covenant was with them that they shouted loud enough to make the ground shake! Here's the catch: the ark wasn't a magic charm. The ark wasn't actually about "the ark" at all. It was about God's presence. The Israelites lost that battle because their confidence was in the object, not in God Himself.

> "When the ark of the covenant of the LORD entered the camp, all the Israelites raised such a loud shout that the ground shook."
> 1 Samuel 4:5 CSB

Let's be grateful that we don't have to carry the ark around to know God is with us. Because of Jesus, His presence isn't in a box—it's in us. His Holy Spirit goes with us, is in us, and all around us. When we truly believe this, we walk differently. We fight differently. We live with confidence.

Where is your confidence? Is it in circumstances, symbols, or people? Or is it in the One who never leaves you?

Prayer:

Lord Jesus, I am so thankful for Your presence. I can't even imagine how much I take this gift for granted. I ask You today to help me truly relish in Your presence and move confidently wherever I go, knowing that You are with me. In Jesus' name. Amen.

1 samuel *five*

The Philistines thought they had won. They took the ark of the covenant like it was a trophy—proof that their gods had defeated Israel's God.

> "The Ekronites called all the Philistine rulers together. They said, 'Send the ark of Israel's God away. Let it return to its place so it won't kill us and our people!' For the fear of death pervaded the city; God's hand was oppressing them."
>
> 1 Samuel 5:11 CSB

But they quickly realized they had no idea what they were messing with. Plagues, panic, and pure chaos followed wherever the ark went. The Philistines couldn't get rid of it fast enough!

What a reminder that God will not be mocked. Even when it looks like the enemy has won, God is never defeated. He will always get the glory.

Prayer:

Lord, help me remember when life seems unfair and evil seems to prevail that You, Lord, are on the throne, and You work in ALL things for my good. In Jesus' name. Amen.

1 samuel six

Before Jesus, no one could stand in God's presence unless they were a priest, set apart, and following strict laws. The average believer could only interact with God through someone else.

> "The people of Beth-shemesh asked, 'Who is able to stand in the presence of the LORD this holy God? To whom should the ark go from here?'"
> 1 Samuel 6:20 CSB

Can you imagine? If you had a question, needed wisdom, or just wanted to feel close to God, you'd have to go through someone else: no personal Bible study, no prayer time, no worship on your own.

Praise the Lord that everything has changed! Because of Jesus, we don't need an earthly priest to stand between us and God. We can be in His presence, talk to Him directly, and hear from Him through His Word—all because of His Holy Spirit living in us.

That's a gift worth celebrating!

Prayer:

Lord, I pray that I never take for granted what Jesus did for me on the cross. Thank You for tearing down every barrier between us and giving me direct access to You. I'm grateful for the church and the body of Christ, but even more, I'm grateful that I can know You personally. Thank You for Your Holy Spirit. In Jesus' name. Amen.

1 samuel seven

On the surface, this looks like the best-case scenario: God showed up, Israel won the battle, their cities were restored, and they had peace. But let's not miss how it happened: God fought for them. It wasn't their strength, their strategy, or their skill that brought victory. It was the Lord's power alone that turned the tide.

> "Samuel was offering the burnt offering as the Philistines approached to fight against Israel. The LORD thundered loudly against the Philistines that day and threw them into such confusion that they were defeated by Israel.
>
> ...
>
> "The cities from Ekron to Gath, which they had taken from Israel, were restored... There was also peace between Israel and the Amorites."
>
> 1 Samuel 7:10, 14 CSB

Still, even in this miraculous moment, their experience of God was limited. He was active, but not yet intimate. Present, but still distant. The Israelites needed prophets and priests to speak to God on their behalf; they didn't have direct access to Him.

But today, because of Jesus Christ, we have something far greater. He doesn't just fight for us—He lives in us. He conquered sin and death forever. He didn't just bring temporary peace. He gave us eternal reconciliation with the Father. And now, because of His Holy Spirit, we carry His presence everywhere we go.

So why would we settle for "good enough"—for going through the motions, checking the boxes, or staying safe in tradition—when we've been invited into daily, intimate communion with the living God?

We don't need a temple—we are the temple. We don't need someone else to speak to God for us—we have direct access. The best of the Old Covenant can't compare to the reality of the New.

Prayer:

Lord, thank You for making it so I don't have to fight my battles alone or settle for a distant relationship with You. You've given me something greater: Your very presence, living inside me. Help me walk in that truth today. I don't want to be lukewarm. I want all that You have for me. In Jesus' name. Amen.

1 samuel *eight*

Oh, Israel—what were you thinking?! You had the one true God leading you, and you'd rather have a human king? It's easy to shake our heads at them, but we often do the same thing.

We want what we want when we want it. We compare, we chase after things God never intended for us, and even when He's shown us over and over that His ways are better than man's, we still think ours might be the exception.

> "And the LORD told him: 'Listen to all that the people are saying to you; it is not you they have rejected, but they have rejected me as their king.'"
> 1 Samuel 8:7 NIV

And the truth? God won't force Himself on us. If we insist on doing things our way, He'll let us. But doing things our way always comes at a cost.

So today, instead of resisting His authority, let's surrender to it because our best ideas don't hold a candle to His perfect plans.

Prayer:

Lord, forgive me for the times I have rejected You as my King, when I've sought my own way instead of surrendering to Yours. It doesn't always feel like self-reliance in the moment, but that's exactly what it is. I don't want to be ruled by my desires; I want to be led by You. Help me fully trust You. In Jesus' name. Amen.

1 samuel nine

Even though the Israelites rejected God as their King, He still had compassion on them. He didn't abandon them. Instead, He provided a king to help them.

> "'About this time tomorrow I will send you a man from the land of Benjamin. Anoint him ruler over my people Israel; he will deliver them from the hand of the Philistines. I have looked on my people, for their cry has reached me.'
>
> "Saul answered, 'But am I not a Benjamite, from the smallest tribe of Israel, and is not my clan the least of all the clans of the tribe of Benjamin? Why do you say such a thing to me?'"
>
> 1 Samuel 9:16, 21 NIV

That doesn't mean they wouldn't face hardship. But it does mean that even in their unfaithfulness, God was still faithful. He was still working for their good.

This is exactly what God does for us as well. He doesn't wait for us to get it all together before stepping in with grace and provision. He is kind, patient, and merciful, even though we don't deserve it.
And if God treats us that way, then shouldn't we extend that same grace to others?

Prayer:

Lord, I am in awe of Your faithfulness. You love me, provide for me, and work in all things for my good, even though I don't deserve it. Help me extend that same grace and kindness to others, treating them according to who I am in You, not what I think they deserve. In Jesus' name. Amen.

1 samuel ten

What an incredible moment this must have been—not just for those who witnessed it but for Saul himself. Imagine the weight of that transformation, the humbling realization that God's Spirit had come upon him and changed him.

> "The Spirit of the LORD will come powerfully upon you, and you will prophesy with them; and you will be changed into a different person. Once these signs are fulfilled, do whatever your hand finds to do, for God is with you."
>
> 1 Samuel 10:6–7 NIV

And the best part? This isn't just Saul's story. It's ours too. As sons and daughters of Christ, we don't have to wish for an encounter like this—we've already had one. The moment we accepted Jesus Christ as our Lord and Savior, the Holy Spirit came to dwell within us and transform us.

May we live in this truth.

Prayer:

Lord, help me grasp the fullness of the gift You've given me through Your Spirit. Teach me to walk in the confidence of who I am in You—fully changed, fully empowered, and fully Yours. May my life reflect the transformation You've already begun in me. In Jesus' name. Amen.

1 samuel eleven

It's fascinating to see Saul at the beginning of his reign—humble, confident, and completely surrendered to the Lord. He had no leadership experience or military background, but he didn't let that stop him. Why? Because his confidence wasn't in himself. It was in God.

> "But Saul said, 'No one will be put to death today, for this day the LORD has rescued Israel.'"
> 1 Samuel 11:13 NIV

Don't you just love how raw and innocent his faith is in this moment?! He knows exactly who is behind the victory, and he doesn't take the credit.

But as you may know, Saul's faith doesn't stay here. Eventually, he stopped trusting God's strength and started relying on his own.

Let's be mindful of this so that we never lose the kind of surrendered confidence that Saul showed in today's reading—the kind of confidence that leads boldly but stays humble. The kind that knows exactly who is in control.

Prayer:

Lord, I want to lead with humility, confidence, and faithfulness in all that You've given me to do. Keep my heart surrendered to You, always remembering that You are the source of my strength, wisdom, and success. May I never drift from trusting You completely. In Jesus' name. Amen.

1 samuel twelve

Often, we read the Old Testament and think, I would never serve false gods! Golden statues? Asherah poles? No way.

But the truth? We usually have idols and false gods of our own—they just look different.

> "Do not turn away after useless idols. They can do you no good, nor can they rescue you, because they are useless."
> 1 Samuel 12:21 NIV

Our gods may not be a carved image, but we may put our trust in money to provide security. Instead of relying on God, we may rely on people, jobs, and our own self-reliance to "save" us. So when we hear warnings like this, let's not just skim past them. Let's ask ourselves, "What am I prioritizing over God?"

Is it your schedule? Your kids? Your own desires?

Prayer:

Lord, keep my heart attentive to anything that tries to take Your place. Help me recognize the subtle ways I rely on things or people more than You. You alone are my Source, my Security, and my Savior. In Jesus' name. Amen.

1 Samuel *thirteen*

When God was Israel's King, no matter how disobedient, fearful, or unfaithful the people were, He remained faithful. But now, under human leadership, we see just how quickly fear can compromise obedience.

> "So he said, 'Bring me the burnt offering and the fellowship offerings.' And Saul offered up the burnt offering."
>
> 1 Samuel 13:9 NIV

Saul was anointed and appointed, but he was still human. And here, we see the breakdown begin—a pattern of compromise that would repeat itself for generations. No matter how powerful or chosen a human king might be, they are still just that—human.

So, let's be grateful that we don't live under the old system. We don't have to rely on an earthly king or priest to stand in the gap for us. Jesus has already done that. His sacrifice put us in right standing with God once and for all.

Prayer:

Lord, I am so thankful that I don't have to live under a broken system. Thank You for Jesus, who made a way for me to live in relationship with You. May I never let fear or impatience compromise my obedience. Help me trust Your timing and Your ways above my own. In Jesus' name. Amen.

1 samuel fourteen

The Israelites begged for a king, believing a human leader would bring them victory, but when the battle came, it wasn't the king who saved them—it was the Lord.

> "So on that day the LORD saved Israel, and the battle moved on beyond Beth Aven."
> 1 Samuel 14:23 NIV

What a powerful reminder that no matter who holds a position of power—whether in government, leadership, or even in our personal lives—God is the one who truly reigns. He alone has the final say. He gives, He takes away, and He goes before us, fighting battles we don't even see.

Prayer:

Lord, help me put my trust in You alone. Remind me that no person, position, or earthly power can replace Your authority in my life. Thank You for going before me, fighting on my behalf, and leading me in every battle. I surrender my fears and plans, knowing that You alone provide the victory. In Jesus' name. Amen.

1 Samuel fifteen

We often say that partial obedience is disobedience, but this passage takes it even further. God equates disobedience with idolatry. It's a sobering reminder that all sin is serious in His eyes.

> "For rebellion is as [serious as] the sin of divination (fortune-telling), And disobedience is as [serious as] false religion and idolatry. Because you have rejected the word of the LORD, He also has rejected you as king."
>
> 1 Samuel 15:23 AMP

Living for God should not be about figuring out where the "line" is. It should be about truly understanding the weight of sin and its effects. Even if we think we get away with something, we never actually do—every sin carries consequences, whether seen or unseen.

It can be difficult to understand why God extends mercy in some situations but brings swift judgment in others. What's important is not that we understand why God does what He does but that we understand sin always takes something from us.

Prayer:

Lord, keep my heart tender toward You. I don't want to drift so far from You that I don't even realize I'm walking in disobedience. Help me see sin for what it really is—not something to manage or justify, but something that separates me from You. Give me a heart that truly seeks You, fully obeys You, and deeply loves You. In Jesus' name. Amen.

1 Samuel sixteen

Don't you just love that we get to see Samuel's humanity here? He was grieving. We're not sure if it was because of disappointment, loyalty, personal preference, or something else, but we know he was struggling to move on.

> "The LORD said to Samuel, 'How long are you going to mourn for Saul, since I have rejected him as king over Israel? Fill your horn with oil and go. I am sending you to Jesse of Bethlehem because I have selected for myself a king from his sons.'"
>
> 1 Samuel 16:1 CSB

Letting go of what we think should happen or how we want things to go can be difficult, especially when our hearts are invested. Just because we love Jesus and want to follow Him doesn't mean we always understand or agree with where He's leading us.

Let's take God's message to Samuel to heart: It's time to stop mourning. Get up and go.

Prayer:

Lord, I don't want to hold onto things You've told me to let go of. Give me the courage to trust You and move forward, even when my heart still wants to stay where it's comfortable. I know Your plans are better than mine, even when it doesn't seem like it in the moment. Help me to pick up my cross, surrender my preferences, and follow You. In Jesus' name. Amen.

1 samuel seventeen

When Saul was first crowned king, he was young, tall, and full of confidence. His confidence wasn't in himself, though; it came from knowing who was backing him. Fast forward, and we see Saul terrified to fight the Philistines—specifically, Goliath. Now, David, another young man, soon to be king, wasn't afraid to fight Goliath. From the outside, he seemed wildly unqualified for this battle, but David's confidence wasn't in his own strength. It was in the Lord.

> "David said to Saul, 'Don't let anyone be discouraged by him; your servant will go and fight this Philistine!'
> "But Saul replied, 'You can't go fight this Philistine. You're just a youth, and he's been a warrior since he was young.'
> ...
> "Then David said, 'The LORD who rescued me from the paw of the lion and the paw of the bear will rescue me from the hand of this Philistine.'
> "Saul said to David, 'Go, and may the LORD be with you.'"
>
> 1 Samuel 17:32–33, 37 CSB

There's something beautiful about youthful, childlike faith—the faith we have before life beats us up and fear begins to creep in. Before we start believing our wins are because of us instead of the Lord.

Let's get back to having that kind of faith.

Prayer:

Lord, help me to have the kind of faith that doesn't hesitate, doubt, or overthink—the kind of faith that remembers it's You who fights for me. Strip away any false confidence I have in myself and replace it with a childlike trust in You. In Jesus' name. Amen.

1 samuel eighteen

David and Saul had quite a bit in common, at least at the beginning.

Both were chosen by God, both were humble, and both questioned whether they were worthy of their callings.

When Saul was first anointed, he responded, "Who am I?" (1 Samuel 9:21). Now, we see David, years later, saying almost the exact same thing.

> "So they told this to David, and he answered, 'It's a great honor to become the king's son-in-law, too great for someone poor and insignificant like me.'"
>
> 1 Samuel 18:23 GNT

They both started in a place of humility, fully aware that their strength came from the Lord. Somewhere along the way, though, Saul's humility turned to pride. The more victories he won, the more he relied on himself instead of the Lord. Success didn't ruin Saul—pride did.

It's easy to look at Saul and think, I would never. The truth is, we all have the potential to let pride creep in. We usually start out depending on God, but when things begin to go well, we don't always give credit where it belongs.

Prayer:

Lord, keep me humble. No matter what success comes my way, help me remember that You are the source of it all. Help me always remember that I need You just as much on the mountaintop as I do in the valley. Keep my heart soft, my confidence in You, and my dependence on You alone. In Jesus' name. Amen.

1 samuel nineteen

Jealousy is a dangerous thing. It starts as insecurity, grows into comparison, and, if left unchecked, can spiral into full-blown destruction. Here, we see that Saul is unraveling. The very man God once chose and anointed to be king is now blinded by envy.

> "Saul told his son Jonathan and all his officials that he planned to kill David. But Jonathan was very fond of David..."
>
> 1 Samuel 19:1 GNT

Saul could not stop what God had already set in motion. The harder he fought against David, the more evident God's protection became. Every attempt Saul made to harm him failed. Every plan backfired. The more he raged, the more foolish he looked—even to the point of losing control, stripping off his robes, and prophesying under God's power (1 Samuel 19:23–24).

That's the thing about God's sovereignty—no human jealousy, insecurity, or opposition can override it. So, why do we waste energy fearing what people might do to us? Why do we stress over their opinions, manipulations, or attempts to bring us down?
If God is for us, nothing and no one can stand against us.

Prayer:

Lord, keep my heart free from pride, jealousy, and fear. Help me trust that no one can take what You have for me. When opposition comes, help me rest in Your sovereignty, knowing that nothing and no one can stop Your plans. In Jesus' name. Amen.

1 samuel twenty

Proverbs tells us that a sweet friendship refreshes the soul (Proverbs 27:9), and it's hard to imagine a sweeter example of this than Jonathan and David.

> "Jonathan asked David to promise again that they would be friends. That was because Jonathan loved David as much as he loved his own life."
> 1 Samuel 20:17 EASY

Friendships come for different seasons—most for a short time and a rare few for a lifetime. But even lifelong friendships don't always look like the level of devotion and loyalty depicted in 1 Samuel 20:17.

Let's not just long for a friend like Jonathan. Let's also strive to be a friend like Jonathan—the kind of friend who is trustworthy, loyal, and unwavering in their love.

Prayer:

Lord, I pray to have and be a friend who is loyal, trustworthy, and godly, just like Jonathan was to David. In Jesus' name. Amen.

1 Samuel *twenty-one*

Everywhere David turned—even when he was on the run—the Lord provided.

> "Ahimelech answered, 'I have the sword of Goliath the Philistine, whom you killed in Elah Valley; it is behind the ephod, wrapped in a cloth. If you want it, take it—it's the only weapon here.'
> "'Give it to me,' David said. 'There is not a better sword anywhere!'"
>
> 1 Samuel 21:9 GNT

It would have been easy for David to feel abandoned, frustrated, or even forgotten. After all, he was God's anointed, yet he was living as a fugitive and being hunted by Saul. But despite the hardship, God's provision never wavered. He kept David safe, gave him loyal people to lead, and even ensured his family was cared for through a neighboring king.

Now that's provision.

We can see the same pattern of provision when we look back on our lives. Even in the seasons when nothing seemed to go the way we wanted, when everything felt uncertain, God still provided, maybe not in the way we expected, but in the way we needed.

Prayer:

Lord, help me recognize Your provision, even when life feels out of control. Give me eyes to see that You are always working, always providing, and always faithful. In Jesus' name. Amen.

1 Samuel *twenty-two*

What started as pride in Saul quickly spiraled into jealousy, anger, and, eventually, paranoia. We can look back and see how Saul got here, but when it comes to our own lives? It's not always so easy to backtrack to where it all started.

> "Then the king said to the guards who stood about him, 'Turn and kill the priests of the LORD, because their hand also is with David, and because they knew when he fled and did not tell it to me.' But the servants of the king would not lift their hands to strike the priests of the LORD."
>
> 1 Samuel 22:17 NKJV

A little pride, a little offense, a little resentment—these "little" things can cause "little" cracks that, if left unchecked, become massive fractures. The Bible warns us not to give the enemy a foothold (Ephesians 4:27) because one seemingly "little" thing can grow into something much bigger than we ever anticipated.

Prayer:

Lord, help me recognize the areas in my life where pride, jealousy, or bitterness try to take root. I don't want to justify or ignore them. I want to surrender them to You before they become massive. Keep my heart soft, my mind clear, and my spirit aligned with You. In Jesus' name. Amen.

1 Samuel twenty-three

Just when it seemed like there was no way out, God made one.

> "Therefore Saul returned from pursuing David, and went against the Philistines; so they called that place the Rock of Escape."
>
> 1 Samuel 23:28 NKJV

David had been running for his life. Every move he made, Saul was right behind him—until, suddenly, a Philistine attack forced Saul to turn back.

David was spared. He didn't have to fight his way out. He didn't have to manipulate or strive because the Lord intervened.

How often do we feel trapped, convinced there's no escape? Maybe it's fear, stress, or circumstances beyond our control. Like David, we can trust that God is already at work, making a way even when we can't see it. The question is, will we trust Him enough to wait?

Prayer:

Lord, when I feel cornered by life's challenges, help me remember that You are my Rock of Escape. You are always working, always making a way. Give me faith to trust You, even when I don't see a way out. In Jesus' name. Amen.

1 Samuel twenty-four

If anyone had a reason to dishonor a leader, it was David. Saul was out for his blood, hunting him down like an enemy instead of recognizing him as the loyal servant he was. Yet, David refused to take matters into his own hands. He honored Saul—not because Saul was honorable, but because God had placed him in a position of authority.

> "He said to his men, 'I pray the LORD never lets me do anything like that to my master again. I must not do anything against Saul, because he is the LORD's chosen king.'"
>
> 1 Samuel 24:6 ERV

How different would the world look today if we followed David's example? The level of disrespect toward leaders—whether in government, workplaces, or even churches—is staggering. The bottom line is this: God appoints and removes leaders. "The authorities that exist have been established by God" (Romans 13:1 NIV).

Whether we agree with them or not, we are called to honor leaders—not because they've earned it, but because we trust God's sovereignty. Honor doesn't mean blind allegiance, but it does mean choosing to respect the position, even when we struggle with the person. David's response to Saul showed his trust in God's timing and justice. Can we say the same about how we respond to our leaders today?

Prayer:

Lord, help me honor those You've placed in authority, even when I disagree with them. Let my words and actions reflect trust in You, not frustration with leadership. Remind me that You are ultimately in control, and help me lead by example in how I speak, act, and pray for those in leadership. In Jesus' name. Amen.

1 Samuel twenty-five

Talk about a close call. Nabal's foolishness brought out the worst in David, but Abigail's wisdom called him to his higher self. She saw the bigger picture and had the courage to step in, keeping David from making a decision he would regret.

> "The people replied, 'We will certainly not abandon the LORD to worship other gods! For the LORD our God brought us and our ancestors out of the land of Egypt, out of the place of slavery, and performed these great signs before our eyes. He also protected us all along the way we went and among all the peoples whose lands we traveled through.'"
>
> 1 Samuel 25:31 ERV

This is iron sharpening iron in action. We all need an Abigail—someone who reminds us who we are and stops us from letting anger or pride lead us into trouble. And wouldn't it be amazing if we could be an Abigail for others as well?

Prayer:

Lord, thank You for the people who have kept me from walking into regret. Help me be an Abigail—bold enough to speak the truth, wise enough to do it with grace, and faithful enough to remind others of who You've called them to be. In Jesus' name. Amen.

1 Samuel *twenty-six*

Saul's words here sound as though maybe he recognized something in David that he had once known for himself but lost. In this moment, Saul validated David—something rare from a king whose jealousy had become a consuming force. For a brief second, Saul acknowledged what God had placed in David. But it would be difficult for Saul to acknowledge David's success without also mourning what he had lost: God's favor, the security of his kingship, and perhaps, his relationship with the Lord.

> "Saul said to David, 'God bless you, my son! You will succeed in everything you do!'
> "So David went on his way, and Saul returned home."
>
> 1 Samuel 26:25 GNT

We can often find ourselves in the same predicament. When we see someone else's success or favor, especially in places we once occupied or desired, it can lead us to resentment or reflection. Saul's words validated David, but they also mirrored his own desires. His recognition of David didn't soften his jealousy; it reflected the pain of what he had failed to protect in his own life: his relationship with God.

Let this be a powerful reminder that jealousy can blind us to the work God is doing in others, and it can open the door to grief if we allow it. Saul's moment of validation should be a warning to us to guard our hearts and avoid becoming bitter toward those whom God has chosen. Let us not mourn what we've lost by failing to follow God's plan. Instead, let's learn from David's faithfulness and move forward, trusting God's plan, regardless of others' jealousy or validation.

Prayer:

Lord, help me recognize the work You are doing in others and guard my heart from the bitterness of comparison. When I feel jealous or insecure, remind me that my value is not found in my position or what I have but in You. May I celebrate Your work in others and trust Your plan for my life, just as David did. In Jesus' name. Amen.

twenty-seven

1 samuel

David, a man after God's own heart, believed his safety lay in the hands of his enemies—the Philistines. Fear clouded his judgment, convincing him that the only way to survive was to flee to enemy territory.

> "But David kept thinking to himself, 'Someday Saul is going to get me. The best thing I can do is escape to the Philistines. Then Saul will stop hunting for me in Israelite territory, and I will finally be safe.'"
>
> 1 Samuel 27:1 NLT

Isn't that how we think sometimes?

How often do we assume that safety means comfort? We tend to believe God's protection looks like familiarity, ease, and certainty, but in reality, His safest place for us might be where we feel the most vulnerable. Maybe for you, that's stepping into fostering or adoption. Maybe it's staying in a secular workplace where you're surrounded by unbelievers. Maybe it's stepping into full-time ministry when it feels like you have nothing to give.

The world tells us certain places are dangerous, uncertain, and unsafe. But our true safety isn't found in our circumstances—it's found in God's perfect plan and presence. David feared Saul, but Saul was never in control of his life. God was.

Let's rest in the truth that the safest place for us is wherever God has called us.

Prayer:

Lord, when fear tempts me to run, remind me that my safety is in You alone. Help me remember that when You call me into the unknown, You are already there. Keep my heart anchored in Your presence so that no matter where I am, I know I am safe in Your hands. In Jesus' name. Amen.

1 Samuel twenty-eight

Saul had everything going for him. He was chosen by God, anointed as king, and given victory after victory. But jealousy crept in, so instead of seeing David as an ally, Saul saw him as a threat. Instead of celebrating God's favor on David, he resented it. And because of that, Saul's greatest warrior—his most loyal asset—was now fighting for the other team.

> "'Of course,' David answered. 'I am your servant, and you will see for yourself what I can do.'
> "Achish said, 'Good! I will make you my permanent bodyguard.'"
>
> 1 Samuel 28:2 GNT

It's devastating, really. Saul's fear, pride, and insecurity blinded him to what was right in front of him. How often do we do the same and let pride, fear, or jealousy keep us from the very people God placed in our lives for our good?

Maybe there's someone in your life right now—a friend, a coworker, a family member—whom you're pushing away because of insecurity. Maybe, like Saul, you're missing out on an incredible ally because your focus is in the wrong place.

Prayer:

Lord, open my eyes. Who am I jealous of? Who am I afraid will outshine me? Who have I let pride push away? I don't want to lose the people You've placed in my life because of my own insecurity. Help me celebrate others, embrace humility, and trust that Your best for me is never threatened by someone else's success. In Jesus' name. Amen.

1 Samuel twenty-nine

Rejection stings. It's confusing, frustrating, and, at times, completely disheartening. David knew that feeling well. He had proven his loyalty to the Philistines time and time again, yet here he was, being sent away. It didn't make sense.

> "'What have I done to deserve this treatment?' David demanded. 'What have you ever found in your servant, that I can't go and fight the enemies of my lord the king?'"
>
> 1 Samuel 29:8 NLT

But what David couldn't see at the moment was that this rejection was actually God's protection. If he had been allowed to fight alongside the Philistines, he would have been battling his own people—the very people he was called to lead as king. What felt like rejection was actually divine intervention.

How often do we feel the same way? We pray, we work hard, we do everything right, but the door still closes. The opportunity still falls through. The relationship still doesn't work out. And we wonder, God, why? What did I do wrong?

But maybe, just maybe, that rejection isn't a punishment—it's protection. Maybe what feels like a disappointment today is actually God keeping us from something that could harm us, mislead us, or take us off course.

Prayer:

Lord, in the moments I feel utterly defeated or left out, help me remember that You are always working behind the scenes for my good and that what feels like rejection is often Your protection or redirection.

Give me faith to trust You, even when I don't understand, and peace to rest in Your perfect plan. In Jesus' name. Amen.

1 samuel *thirty*

One of the greatest things about David's leadership wasn't just his courage or skill in battle—it was his dependence on God. Before making a move, he sought the Lord's counsel. He didn't assume, react, or rely solely on his own wisdom. He asked the Lord what he should do. And because of that, he moved forward with clarity and confidence.

> "Then David asked the LORD, 'Should I chase after this band of raiders? Will I catch them?'
> "And the LORD told him, 'Yes, go after them. You will surely recover everything that was taken from you!'"
>
> 1 Samuel 30:8 NLT

How often do we make decisions without stopping to seek God's guidance? We rush into action, react emotionally, and lean on our own understanding. But what if, like David, we paused and asked, "Lord, what is Your strategy? What is Your will in this situation?"

We have God's Holy Spirit living inside us! He is our Counselor, our Guide, and the One who reveals God's wisdom in every situation. There is nothing too big or too small for Him. He cares about our battles, our decisions, and even our daily struggles. And when we seek His perspective, He gives us the strategy, wisdom, and confidence to move forward.

Prayer:

Lord, thank You for the gift of Your guidance. Help me to pause and seek Your strategy before I react or make decisions. Holy Spirit, lead me so that I walk in Your wisdom and not my own. In Jesus' name. Amen.

1 Samuel thirty-one

What a tragic ending to Saul's life. A king who once stood tall and full of promise was consumed by fear and despair. Saul's fall is a reminder that no matter how high a person rises, it's only by God's hand that they remain.

> "Saul told the boy who carried his armor, 'Take your sword and kill me or else these foreigners will do it and torment me as well!' But Saul's helper was afraid and refused to kill him. So Saul took out his own sword and fell on it."
>
> 1 Samuel 31:4 ERV

You might be feeling the weight of all that's happening in our world today. Political tensions are at an all-time high. People are divided, frustrated, and angry, and lines are being drawn on every issue. You may look at the leaders in power and wonder where God's hand is.

Let your confidence rest in this: God is still on the throne. Saul's story is a reminder that God's sovereignty is not dependent on human leadership. Whether our leaders acknowledge Him or not, God's control over all things remains unchanged. We might not understand the politics, the decisions, or the unrest around us, but we can rest in the confidence that God is still in control.

Prayer:

Lord, in times of chaos and confusion, help me remember that You are still on the throne. Help me trust in Your sovereignty, knowing that nothing happens outside of Your will. Give me peace in the midst of unrest and confidence in Your plan. In Jesus' name. Amen.

Women @the well
Meet the Authors

Kami

Kami is a former teacher and basketball coach who has transformed her passion for mentoring into a thriving career as an entrepreneur and real estate professional. Based in sunny Southwest Florida, she's the proud mother of five amazing children—two of whom she adopted after moving from Michigan following a divorce. Kami's days are filled with sports events, family activities, and juggling her many roles, from taxi driver to advocate for women and youth. Off the clock, you'll often find her on the pickleball court, where her competitive spirit truly comes alive!

copyright notice

No part of this publication may be reproduced, stored, or transmitted in any form or by any means, electronic, mechanical, photocopying, recording, scanning, or otherwise, except as permitted under Section 107 or 108 of the 1976 United States Copyright Act, without the prior written permission of the author.

Limitation of liability/disclaimer of warranty: While the publisher and author have used their best efforts in preparing this workbook, they make no representations or warranties with respect to the accuracy or completeness of the contents of this document and specifically disclaim any implied warranties of merchantability or fitness for a particular purpose. No warranty may be created or extended by sales representatives, promoters, or written sales materials.

The advice and strategies contained herein may not be suitable for your situation. You should consult with a professional where appropriate. Neither the publisher nor author shall be liable for any loss of profit or any other commercial damages, including but not limited to special, incidental, consequential, or other damages.

ISBN: 979-8-9920878-5-7
All Original Content Is Copyrighted by The Well Encounter. LLC
thewellencounter.com| @ 2023 The Well Encounter

We hope you continue this journey with us. Our next devotional is
Manna in the Morning: History - Volume 2.

www.ingramcontent.com/pod-product-compliance
Lightning Source LLC
LaVergne TN
LVHW021117080426
835512LV00011B/2554